MW00901230

SPANISH AT HOME

¡Aprendemos en familia!©

Ready-to-use activities and tools to boost your Spanish at home.

INDEX

More than 50 interactive activities for 0-6 years old to bring Spanish into your family life.

safeCreative
1801035261676
INFO ABOUT RIGHTS

I edición digital 30 de diciembre de 2017.
Autoras: **Erica** Mirochnik (www.**mamasporelmundo**.com), **Minerva** Ortega (www.**retobilingue**.com), **Elizabeth** García (www.**infanciayeducacion**.com)

PROLOGUE

The goal of this book is to inspire you to start the adventure of bilingualism. It's based on the idea that learning a second language is the most incredible gift you can give to your children.

There are many ways to do this; but the most important thing is to take the first big step along the path of bilingualism; to recognize its importance in your child's education and be committed to the idea that a new language brings richness to your house and better prepares your child for the multicultural world we live in. Indeed, knowing a language gives you access to different cultures from which you can learn and benefit.

In practical terms, knowing more than one language opens doors in education and employment, because it broadens the possibilities of interaction and knowledge and provides a skill that is increasingly valuable in the global marketplace.

Starting this journey can be daunting, but fear not! we have compiled a set of activities and resources to bring Spanish to your life in an easy, fun and interactive way.

Enjoy!

Erica, Minerva & Elizabeth

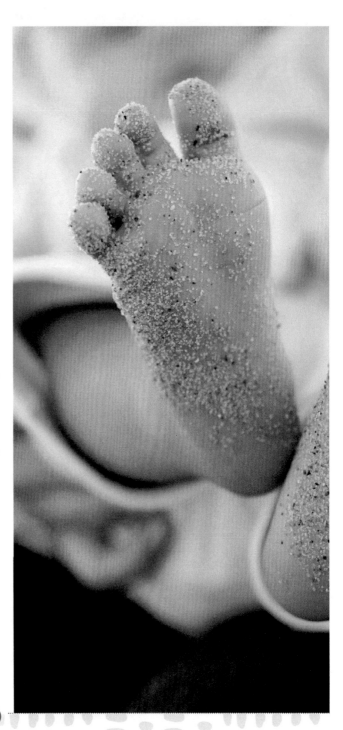

3

WHO WE ARE

Erica Mirochnik ·

My name is Erica, I am originally from Argentina. I am an educational psychologist and an expatriate consultant. I have lived abroad with my family for 20 years, in cities such as Paris, Montreal and now I live in New York. My daily life, my feelings and my profession are largely conditioned by distance, by the new cultures that I have known and the experiences that have allowed me to grow personally and professionally.

Learning new languages has been critical in our lives as we moved around the world. We managed to keep Spanish as a mother tongue at home while incorporating the local languages to our professionals and educational lives. We have raised our multilingual children in the idea of respect between cultures. Knowing different languages enriches our lives in an unpredictable way. Our kids are fluent in 3 languages and enjoy the different aspects of each of them.

In our family, we are strong believers in the importance of multilingualism. We see it as a tool for life and a vehicle to know different cultures and outlooks. We worked hard towards instilling that value in our children, who proudly define themselves as multi-lingual and multi-cultural.

This book is part of this journey and it's nourished by the experiences of many families who share and value bilingual education. It is a way to get closer to those who want to embark in this adventure. Bilingual education is a challenge to be taken seriously in order to enjoy the advantages it offers.

Many of these ideas have also been shared in my consulting agency, Mamás por el Mundo. To learn more I invite you to visit **www.mamasporelmundo.com**

Minerva Ortega

Hello! My name is Minerva and I'm a Mexican who, for the last 10 years has been living between México and the United States. I am a professional engineer, but I believe my real call is in the field of education. The moment I knew that I was pregnant with my son, I made the vow to raise him bilingual, and that both Spanish and English would be part of his life from day one. Watching my son learn vocabulary in English from videos designed to teach while playing, I decided to develop a similar method to teach Spanish. In 2016, I founded Tots Playtime, a series of educational videos in Spanish for kids.

Most recently, I started Reto Bilingüe, **www.retobilingue.com** a blog for parents that promotes bilingualism all over the world. The blog includes video podcasts with resources, tips, personal experiences from bilingual or multilingual families, and the input of experts on the subject.

Today, I'm a proud mom of a fully bilingual boy. At the age of 3, he started to have conversations in both languages, holding his own with native speakers. I believe the key to success in learning languages is the combination of good resources and daily practice. .

Enjoy this book, it offers a lot of resources for your little ones. My best advice: have fun, enjoy speaking with your kid, play a lot, and create a fun environment for the love of languages to blossom.

Elizabeth García ·

Hi there! My name is Elizabeth. I am an educator, and I feel great passion for my profession! For the last ten years, I have grown professionally and personally, working on educational projects with kids and adults. Of course, my growth accelerated when I became a mom in 2013 and then again in 2015. I was born in New Jersey and grew up in Madrid, Spain. I moved back to the States with my husband in 2012. I worked in a lovely school as a Spanish teacher in Austin, Texas for five years. Our two children were born there, a boy and girl that are now 4 and 2.

Today you will find me in Seville, Spain, where we live since June 2017. Although English is our second language, we are raising our kids bilingual. Furthermore, here in Spain it's hard to find English speaking friends for the kids to practice regularly... But our beautiful experience in Austin and the good memories we carry from our life across the Ocean have made our brain and our heart bilingual, so we won't give up!

I am so glad you are reading this book, and I hope you'll engage with the useful resources that we are offering here. There are no shortcuts or magic formulas... The first step is to create positive experiences in Spanish and the rest will come. This book will help you do just that!

I write about childhood and education on my blog **www.infanciayeducacion.com**.

I hope that somehow our paths cross on this unpredictable and magic journey.

INTRODUCTION

INTRODUCTION

Since the 1960s, numerous scientific publications have proven the benefits of beginning learning a second language at an early age.

Authors such as Penfield and Roberts (1959) and Lenneberg (1967) explain that early childhood – when children are acquiring their mother tongue – is a critical time to begin the process of learning a second language.

Studies show that if children come into contact with the second language in a natural, stable and continuous way, from birth to approximately three years old, they will acquire it simultaneously to the mother tongue. This early interaction with the second language offers better possibilities of mastering it, compared to children that have not benefited from that early exposure.

In addition, different authors refer to neurobiological, cognitive, emotional, motivational and personality-related factors of the child, as decisive in the process of learning a second language.

In today's world, acquiring a second language can play a key role in one's professional and personal growth...

However, learning a language is a complex process. The factors that influence this process are many and varied, so talking about magic recipes or rapid results does not make much sense.

Learning a second language requires emotion, exposure, practice, time and patience. The good news is that the tools we have at our disposal make it easier for our children to acquire the language in a playful, meaningful and affordable way!

For true learning to happen, our heart and our brain need to get on board. So either because you have several languages in your heart or because learning a second language is exciting and you want to live this adventure as a family, do not forget that learning languages is a matter of identity, cultural diversity, respect, expression of ideas and feelings and above all the connection with other people. There is no greater "success" than seeing the family enjoying the learning process together over time and no greater richness than exposing our children to other people's cultures.

Some important things to consider:

- Learning a second language is much more than learning words in another language.
- It is important to be clear about what motivates your family and find the methods that work best for you.
- If we have decided that it is a priority in the education of our children, it is necessary to accompany them and commit ourselves to this process for the long run.

SPANISH AT HOME · Erica Mirochnik · Minerva Ortega · Elizabeth García

- The use of the second language must be included in the family routines.

- The sooner you start your exposure to the second language, the better!

- Our role as parents is to promote a positive attitude towards the acquisition of the second language and to make available the resources that we consider most appropriate to the learning process.

- The parents' level of proficiency in the language is an important factor that influences the learning process of the children but is not determining.

- It is important to manage our expectations and not become obsessed with short-term results. Children should enjoy learning a language without stress.

- The family, the school and the environment play a fundamental role in the child's learning process. The commitment to this process starts at home.

- A language that is not regularly practiced is easily forgotten.

SCOPE AND METHODOLOGY

This document is geared towards non-native adults with an intermediate level of Spanish, raising children between zero and six years old.

We give you ideas, suggestions, and tools to make the process of introducing this beautiful language to your kids easier and more effective, while you learn it at the same time.

Among the support materials that we recommend, you will find popular resources that you probably know in English, and are available in Spanish too. There are also specific resources commonly used in Spanish Speaking Countries that you can get through online stores.

Learning a second language is not an easy task so it is better if you include Spanish in your daily routines in a playful and enjoyable way. You can start using Spanish while playing, reading stories or listening to audio books during the bath time or cooking. It is important for you to start with confidence and decision.

The uniqueness of Spanish at home! Aprendemos en familia lies in its playful approach and "coming together" learning process. It is about choice, love, respect, confidence, persistence, effort, improvement and acceptance.

Hopefully this is just the beginning of a wonderful experience. Let's begin!

SPANISH IS THE OFFICIAL LANGUAGE IN 21 COUNTRIES

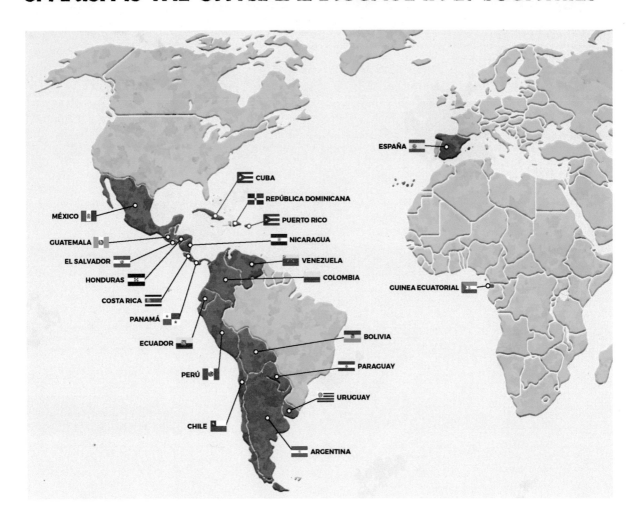

According to the report of the Instituto Cervantes "El español: Una lengua viva":

- In 2016, more than 472 million people have Spanish as their mother tongue.
- 7.8% of the world's population speaks Spanish
- Spanish is the second mother tongue in the world by number of speakers.
- For demographic reasons, the percentage of the world's population that speaks Spanish as a native language is increasing.
- More than 21 million students learn Spanish as a foreign language.

♫ MUSIC

 **MUSIC**

MUSIC & AUTHORS OF MUSIC IN SPANISH

Author/Name	Country	Website
Francisco Gabilondo Soler " El grillo cantor"	México	www.cricri.com.mx
Andrés Salguero " 123 Andres"	Colombia	www.123andres.com
Nathalia bilingual kids music	Colombia	www.nathaliamusic.com
Rockalingua	Spain /United States	www.rockalingua.com
Mundo Lanugo	Dominican Republic / Estados Unidos	www.mundolanugo.com
La gallina pintadita	Brazil	www.gallinapintadita.com
Juana la Iguana	United States	www.juanalaiguana.com
Cánticos	United States	www.canticosworld.com
Los Musiqueros	Argentina	www.losmusiqueros.com
Canticuénticos	Argentina	www.canticuenticos.com.ar

SPANISH AT HOME · Erica Mirochnik · Minerva Ortega · Elizabeth García

 # MUSIC

TRADITIONAL SONGS & LYRICS

Author/Name	Country	Songs
José Luis Orozco	México	• Buenos días • El Chocolate • La araña pequeñita • Los Elefantes
Francisco Gabilondo Soler	México	• Tema de Cri-Cri • Caminito de la escuela • Ratón Vaquero • La marcha de las letras • El chorrito
Miliki	Spain	• Mi barba tiene tres pelos • Susanita tiene un ratón • La Gallina Turuleta
Fernando García Morcillo	Spain	• Mi vaca lechera
Popular songs	Spain/México/Argentina	• Estrellita del lugar • La Vaca Lola • En la granja de mi tío... • El Señor Don Gato • A mi burro enfermo
Maria Elena Walsh	Argentina	• Osías el osito • Manuelita la tortuga • Canción de tomar el té • El reino del revés
Pipo Pescador	Argentina	• El auto de papá • Marcha de los Anti sopas • Tren de Aserrín

SPANISH AT HOME · Erica Mirochnik · Minerva Ortega · Elizabeth García

TRADITIONAL MEXICAN SONGS

Acitrón de un fandango

Juego en círculo

Acitrón de un fandango,

Zango, zango, sabaré,

Sabaré que va pasando,

Con su triqui, triqui, tran.

Por la calle voy pasando,

Por la vía pasa el tren,

Acitrón de un fandango,

Zango, zango, sabaré.

Antonio tenía una flauta,

Con ella se divertía

Y vamos a dar la lata

A la casa de su tía,

Con su triqui, triqui, tran.

A la víbora, víbora de la mar, de la mar

Por aquí pueden pasar.

Los de adelante corren mucho,

Los de atrás se quedarán,

Tras, tras, tras.

Una Mexicana, que frutas vendía,

Ciruelas, chabacanos, melón y sandía.

Verbena, verbena,

Jardín de matatena.

Que llueva, que llueva,

La Virgen de la cueva.

Campanita de oro,

Déjame pasar, con todos mis hijos,

Menos éste de atrás, tras, tras, tras,

Será melón, será sandía

Será la vieja del otro día!

Una rata vieja

Una rata vieja que era planchadora

por planchar su falda se quemó la cola

se puso pomada y se amarró un trapito

y a la pobre rata le quedó un rabito

lero lero lero

lero lero la

esa rata vieja no sabe planchar.

Zapatito blanco, zapatito azul

Zapatito blanco, zapatito azul.

Dime, ¿cuántos años tienes tú?

¡Cinco! 1, 2, 3, 4, 5*

Y sales tú con la letra doble-u.

MUSIC

A mi burro

A mi burro, a mi burro
Le duele la cabeza,
El médico le ha puesto
Una corbata negra.

Una corbata negra,
Mi burro enfermo está,
Mi burro enfermo está.

A mi burro, a mi burro
Le duele la garganta,
El médico le ha puesto
Una bufanda blanca,

Una bufanda blanca,
Una corbata negra,
Mi burro enfermo está,
Mi burro enfermo está.

A mi burro, a mi burro
Le duelen las orejas,
El médico le ha puesto
Una gorrita negra.

Una gorrita negra,
Una bufanda blanca,
Una corbata negra,
Mi burro enfermo está,
Mi burro enfermo está.

A mi burro, a mi burro
Le duelen las pezuñas,
El médico le ha puesto
Emplasto de lechuga.

Emplasto de lechuga,
Una gorrita negra,
Una bufanda blanca,
Una corbata negra,
Mi burro enfermo está,
Mi burro enfermo está.

A mi burro, a mi burro
Le duele el corazón
El médico le ha dado
Jarabe de limón.

Jarabe de limón,
Emplasto de lechuga,
Una gorrita negra,
Una bufanda blanca,
Una corbata negra,
Mi burro enfermo está,
Mi burro enfermo está.

A mi burro, a mi burro
Ya no le duele nada
El médico le ha dado
Jarabe de manzana.

Jarabe de manzana,
Jarabe de limón,
Emplasto de lechuga,
Una gorrita negra,
Una bufanda blanca,
Una corbata negra,
Mi burro enfermo está,
Mi burro enfermo está

SPANISH AT HOME · Erica Mirochnik · Minerva Ortega · Elizabeth García

 # MUSIC

 ## TRADITIONAL SONGS FROM SPAIN

La araña pequeñita

La araña pequeñita
subió, subió, subió.
Vino la lluvia y se la llevó
Salió el sol y todo lo secó
Y la araña pequeñita
subió, subió, subió.

Cinco Lobitos

Cinco lobitos tiene la loba,
cinco lobitos, detrás de la
escoba.
Cinco lobitos, cinco parió,
cinco crió, y a los cinco,
a los cinco tetita les dio.

La Vaca Lola

La vaca Lola

La vaca Lola

Tiene cabeza y

tiene cola y hace así

muuuuuuu

Estrellita del Lugar

Estrellita dónde estás
me   pregunto   quién
serás...
Estrellita dónde estás
me pregunto quién serás.
En el cielo o en el mar
un díamante de verdad.
Estrellita dónde estás
me pregunto quién serás.
Estrellita dónde estás
me pregunto quién serás.
Estrellita dónde estás
me pregunto quién serás.
En el cielo o en el mar
un díamante de verdad.
Estrellita dónde estás
me pregunto quién serás.

Buenos Días

Buenos días, Buenos días,
¿cómo estás? ¿cómo estás?
Muy bien gracias, muy bien,
gracias
¿y usted? ¿y usted?
Buenas tardes, Buenas
tardes
¿cómo estás? ¿cómo estás?
Muy bien gracias, muy bien,
gracias
¿y usted? ¿y usted?
Buenas noches, buenas
noches
¿cómo estás? ¿cómo estás?
Muy bien gracias, muy bien,
gracias
¿y usted? ¿y usted?

Los Elefantes

Un elefante se
balanceaba
sobre la tela de una
araña
Como veía que no se
caía
fue a buscar otro
elefante.
Dos elefantes se
balanceaban
sobre la tela de una
araña
Como veían que no se
caían
Fueron a buscar otro
elefante
Tres elefantes...
Cuatro elefantes...

 # MUSIC

 ## TRADITIONAL SONGS FROM ARGENTINA

Canción del tallarín

Un tallarín, un tallarín

que se mueve por aquí

que se mueve por allá

todo pegoteado

con un poco de aceite

con un poco de sal

Y te lo comes tú

A mi mono le gusta la lechuga

A mi mono, le gusta la lechuga

planchadita sin una sola arruga

se la come, con sal y con limón

muy contento, sentado en mi balcón.

Cara col-col-col

Caracol, -col, -col,

Saca tus cuernos al sol,

Saca uno, saca dos,

Caracol, -col, -col.

Si saca la cabeza y los cuernitos

Cuando hay sol,

Seguro que es un bicho

Que se llama caracol.

Caracol, -col, -col,

Saca tus cuernos al sol,

Saca uno, saca dos,

Caracol, -col, -col.

Al paso, al trote

En un caballo gris,

(nombre del niño/a) se fue a París,

al paso, al trote.

¡al galope, galope, galope!

 **MUSIC**

HAPPY BIRTHDAY SONGS IN SPANISH

Cumpleaños feliz

Country: Spain

Cumpleaños Feliz, Cumpleaños Feliz
Te deseamos todos, Cumpleaños Feliz
Es un muchacho (muchacha) excelente, es
un muchacho excelente, es un muchacho
excelente y siempre lo será, y siempre lo
será y siempre lo será.

Que los cumplas feliz

Country: Argentina

Que los cumplas feliz, que los cumplas feliz,
que los cumplas (nombre del niño/a)
que los cumplas feliz!

La piñata

Country: México

Dale, dale, dale,
No pierdas el tino,
Porque si lo pierdes
Pierdes el camino

Ya le diste una
Ya le diste dos
Ya le diste tres
¡y tu tiempo se acabó!

Las mañanitas

Country: México

Estas son las mañanitas
que cantaba el rey David
Hoy por ser día de tu santo
te las cantamos aquí.
Despierta mi bien despierta
Mira que ya amaneció
Ya los pajaritos cantan
La luna ya se metió.
¡Qué linda está la mañana
en que vengo a saludarte
Venimos todos con gusto
y placer a felicitarte!
El día en que tú naciste,
nacieron todas las flores
Ya viene amaneciendo
ya la luz del día nos dio.
Levántate de mañana,
mira que ya amaneció.
Y En la pila del bautismo
cantaron los ruiseñores.
Ya viene amaneciendo
ya la luz del día nos dio.
Levantarte de la mañana,
mira que ya amaneció.

SPANISH AT HOME · Erica Mirochnik · Minerva Ortega · Elizabeth García

ACTIVITIES & GAMES

ACTIVITIES FOR KIDS 0 TO 3 YRS OLD

JUEGO ADENTRO Y AFUERA - IN & OUT GAME

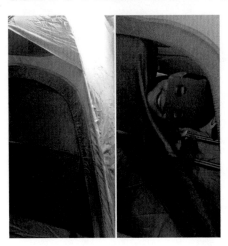

Learning objectives:

language, social skills, gross motor skills and exploring their environment.

Materials needed:

Playhouse or large cardboard box or play tunnel.

Instructions:

Create a cardboard box house, play tunnel, or playhouse. Include an entrance and exit.

- Encourage your child to go in and out.
- Encourage them to copy what you're doing, and then try to copy what they're doing.
- Create a conversation.

Vocabulary:

Tan, Tan, Tan, Tan.	Knock the door
Hola! ¿Hay alguien en casa?	Hello! Is anybody home?
¿Quién es?	Who is it?
¿Puedo pasar?	May I come in?
¡Claro! pasa	Of course! come in
Adentro	Inside
Vamos a jugar a dentro de la casa.	Let's play together inside the house
Ahora vamos a salir.	Now let's get out!
Afuera	Outside
Ahora vamos a hacerlo otra vez.	Now let's do it again

FIESTA EN EL ARENERO - SAND PARTY

Learning objectives:

language, creative play, fine motor skills, tactile stimulation, and social development.

Materials needed:

Sand, buckets, spoons, plastic shovels, and large sand box.

Instructions:

- Encourage your child to dig, pour and scoop.
- Encourage them to copy what you're doing, and then try to copy what they're doing.
- Create a conversation.

Vocabulary:

¡Vamos al arenero!	Let's go to the sandbox
Entra al arenero	Get into the sandbox
¿Qué tal se siente la arena?	How do you feel the sand?
¿Está caliente o fría?	Is it hot or cold?
¿Hacemos un castillo?	Do we make a castle?
Ok, tráeme la cubeta	Ok, bring me the bucket
con la pala meteremos arena a la cubeta	with the shovel we will put sand in the bucket
vamos a llenar la cubeta de arena	let's fill it up with sand
aplanamos la arena dentro de la cubeta	we flatten the sand inside the bucket
vaciamos la cubeta	we pour the sand
¡Muy bien! lo haces muy bien	Very good! you do it very well
Ahora pondremos una bandera al castillo	Now we will put a flag to the castle
Una hoja puede ser nuestra bandera	a leaf can be our flag
inserta la hoja	insert the leaf
¡Listo! nuestro castillo está terminado	Ready! Our castle is finished

LLAMADA POR TELÉFONO - TELEPHONE CALL

Learning objectives:

language and social development skills.

Materials needed:

Toy telephone or old phone.

Instructions:

Hand a phone to your child and keep one for yourself.

* Pretend to make calls, and hold conversations with each other or imaginary people.
* Encourage them to copy what you're doing, and then try to copy what they're doing.
* Create a conversation and ask him to repeat, use funny voices, and create silly characters on the other line.

Vocabulary:

Ring, Ring, Ring!	Ring, Ring, Ring!
¡Bueno! / ¡Hola! / ¡Diga!	Hello!
Soy - XXXX- ¿Cómo has estado?	It's - XXXX- How's it going?
Muy bien	I'm fine and you?
Gracias por preguntar	Thank you for asking
¿Qué estás haciendo?	What are you doing?
Estoy jugando	I'm playing
Me tengo que ir	I have to go
¡Adios!	Bye

SACO UNA MANITO - DANCING HANDS

Learning objectives:

Introducing first words.

Instructions:

As you sing "Saco una manito" with the appropriate gestures, making special emphasis in the words: abro, cierro, guardar, manito, mano, una, dos, bailar. This is an activity that you can also use during meal time.

Vocabulary:

Una manito o una manita	A hand
Saco una manito. La hago bailar	I take out one hand. I make it dance.
La cierro, la abro y la vuelvo a guardar.	I close it, I open it, and I put it away again.
Saco otra manito. La hago bailar	I take out the other hand. I make it dance.
La cierro, la abro y la vuelvo a guardar.	I close it, I open it, and I put it away again.
Saco las dos manitos. Las hago bailar,	I take out two hands. I make them dance.
Las cierro, las abro y las vuelvo a guardar.	I close them, I open them, and I put them away again.

EL JUEGO DE ADIVINAR - THE GUESSING GAME

Learning objectives:

Enrich vocabulary, develop the sense of touch.

Materials needed:

one medium bag, a small ball, a doll, a car, your child's favorite toy, a book, an apple, a spoon, etc.

Instructions:

Place everyday objects in a bag. Choose one without showing it, place the child's hand in the bag so he/she can start feeling and guessing which object it is. Give easy clues to your child, who will then try to guess the item. Play with the words, how the name of the object sounds in Spanish and English. If your child cannot guess or if he/she feels too anxious, change the game, put him in charge and be the one guessing.

Vocabulary:

Doll	muñeca
Ball	balón
Car	auto
Apple	manzana
Book	libro
Spoon	cuchara

BOLICHE O BOLOS - BOWLING

Learning objectives:

Fine and gross motor skills, coordination, concentration, Spanish vocabulary.

Materials needed:

Fariety of balls, 6 or more bowling pins (you can also use any Pringles box or milk cartons and decorate them with your child).

Instructions:

Play a regular bowling game adding the following:

- Name the objects in Spanish
- Allow throwing and kicking the ball
- Count the pins in Spanish
- Put stickers of characters in each pin

ACTIVITIES & GAMES

OTHER EASY GAMES FOR BABIES & TODDLERS

Cucú- tras

This would be the Spanish version of Peek-a-boo. Put yourself in front of your baby and say Hola xxx (the name of your son/daughter). Then cover your face with your hands and ask him/her: Cucú ¿Dónde está mamá? or Cucú ¿Dónde está papá? And when your baby is trying to touch your hands, uncover your face and say: ¡Aquí!

Vocabulario/Vocabulary: Hola/Hello; ¿Dónde está mamá?/Where's mom?; ¿Dónde está papá?/Where is dad?; Aquí/Here.

Palmas palmitas

Play with your baby using your hands and singing this song while giving gentle claps:

"Palmas palmitas, higos y castañitas, azúcar y turrón para mi niño (o para mi niña) son" and end up tickling your baby all over his/her body.

Vocabulario/Vocabulary:Palmada/Clap; Higos/Figs; Castañitas/ (little) Chestnuts; azúcar/ sugar; turrón/ nougat; niño o niña/boy or girl.

Al paso, al trote y al galope

Place your baby on your knees and while riding like a horse sing: "Al paso, al paso, al paso... (you sing slowly) al trote, al trote, al trote (with rhythm) al galope, al galope, al galope (fast, fast, fast!)" making him ride ever more intensely. And back to start.

Vocabulario/Vocabulary: Paso/Pace; Trote/Trot; Galope/Gallop.

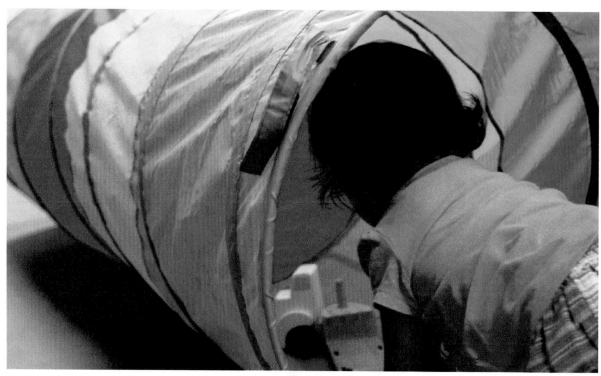

Marionetas de dedo

Choose characters you like (animals, story characters, family members) to make your own puppets, or buy them, and tell simple stories in Spanish with the protagonists placed on your fingers or fingers of your child.

Vocabulario/Vocabulary: Marionetas de dedo/ Finger Puppet

Instrumentos musicales

Flute, Xylophone, Maracas, Drum... there are many instruments you can use with the little one saying the corresponding term in Spanish and singing the songs that we suggest in the section of Music.

Vocabulario/Vocabulary: Instrumentos musicales/ Musical Instruments; Flauta/Flute; Xilófono/Xylophone; Maracas/Maracas;Tambor/ Drum.

Juguetes

Any of the baby toys, as well as the older children, can be a perfect excuse to sit down and play with our baby or toddler and create simple díalogues in Spanish giving life to their favorite characters.

Vocabulario/Vocabulary: Juguetes/Toys; Personaje/Character; Escenarios/ Scenes; Casa/ House; Selva/Jungle; Mar/ Sea; Cielo/Sky; Río/ River.

Construcción con bloques

Creating towers with pieces of wood or other safe materials is a fun activity that allows us to count in Spanish at the same time that we add elements to our construction. We can also create scenarios with which to later play with toys creating new dialogues and stories in Spanish.

Vocabulario/Vocabulary: Construcción con bloques/ Building Blocks; Madera/Wood; Edificio/Building.

Anillos apilables

When our child is already six months, we can play with stacking rings. It is a fun way to stimulate visual motor skills and promote the child's contact with new shapes and textures. It is a perfect plan to practice expressions like "Es tu turno", "Es mi turno","¡Lo conseguiste!"

Vocabulario/Vocabulary: Anillos apilables/ Stacking Rings; Es tu turno/it's your turn; Es mi turno/ it's my turn; Lo conseguiste/You got it!

Juego de cartas

Flashcards about different themes in Spanish help adults practice with children common words that we don't have the chance to use in our daily routine.

Vocabulario/Vocabulary: Juego de cartas/ Flashcards.

Puzzles

Around two years old, start playing simple puzzles and practice easy sentences like "Esta pieza va aquí" "¿Dónde está la pieza con (descripción)?", "¡Mira! "Ya casi lo tenemos" "Lo hicimos" fits here This piece goes here

Vocabulario/Vocabulary: Esta pieza va aquí/ This piece goes here; Casi lo logramos/We almost made it; ¡Lo logramos! / We made it!

Disfraces

The possibilities are endless; we recommend a DIY costumes as a part of the activity.

Vocabulario/Vocabulary: Disfraz/Custome

SPANISH AT HOME · Erica Mirochnik · Minerva Ortega · Elizabeth García

ACTIVITIES FOR KIDS 4 TO 6 YRS OLD

CONSTRUIR CON TUBOS DE PAPEL HIGIÉNICO - BUILD IT UP: TOILET ROLL ACTIVITY

Learning objectives:

language and fine motor skills.

Materials needed:

- toilet paper rolls or cardboard rolls from craft shop
- stickers, coloured paper, magazine paper or confetti
- glue
- scissors
- paints and brushes (optional)
- tape (optional)

Instructions:

- This activity is good for toddlers and preschool children.
- Decorate the rolls with stickers or paper shapes stuck on with tape or glue.
- Allow to dry.
- Little hands can work on creating colorful structures of different heights.

Vocabulary:

Escoge la decoración para los tubos	Choose decoration for the tubes
pega las calcomanías en los tubos	paste the stickers on the tubes
recorta el papel en círculos	cut out the paper in circles
pon pegamento en los círculos	put glue in the circles
pega el círculo en el tubo	stick the circle on the tube
también puedes recortar otras figuras	you can also cut out other figures
cuadrados, triángulos, óvalos	squares, triangles, ovals
al terminar de decorar los ponemos a secar	when we finish decorating we put them to dry
ahora los apilaremos para formar figuras.	now we will build up figures.

GLOBO CON MASA MOLDEABLE - MAKE A PLAY DOUGH WACKY SACK

Learning objectives:

language and fine motor skills.

Materials needed:

- 1 balloon
- 1 tube of play dough per balloon
- glue
- permanent marker

Optional:

- Pom poms
- Googly eyes
- Pipe cleaners
- Yarn

Instructions:

- First you get out your Playdough (I used one container of Playdough per balloon)
- Roll it out into a tube. Then stuff the Playdough inside the balloon.
- Press down on the balloon to get all of the air bubbles out.
- Tie it off.
- Decorate your wacky sack however you'd like!

Vocabulary:

Aplana la plastilina o masa en una línea larga, como si fuera un churro.	Roll out your play dough into a long, thin line
Estira el globo lo más ancho posible y rellena con la plastilina o masa.	Stretch your balloon as wide as you can and stuff the play dough inside.
Presiona el globo relleno lo más plano posible para sacar el aire	Press the filled balloon to make it flat and get as much air out as possible
Amarralo con un nudo	Tie it off with a knot.
Agrega una cara con los ojos locos o dibújalos con el marcador	Add a face using your Googly eyes or draw them with the permanent marker
Agrega el cabello con pegando los limpia pipas o estambre o pompones	Add a hair using your Pipe cleaners, Yarn or pompoms

SPANISH AT HOME · Erica Mirochnik · Minerva Ortega · Elizabeth García

LA ORUGA MUY HAMBRIENTA DE CARTÓN

Learning objectives:

language and fine motor skills.

Materials needed:

- 1 row of egg cups from an egg carton
- red paint
- green paint
- 2 googly craft eyes
- 1 small piece black pipe cleaner
- glue

Instructions:

Cut a row of egg cups from the carton and let them loose with the paints. You can then use it as a prop while you're reading Eric Carle's classic, The Very Hungry Caterpillar.

Activity

Cut a row of six egg cups from the carton. Trim the cups using a craft knife so you get a nice caterpillar shape. Use green paint for the body and red paint for the head.

Glue on the googly eyes. Pierce two holes on the top of the caterpillar's head. Form a small piece of pipe cleaner into a 'V' shape and thread it through the holes, so it pokes up as antenna.

Vocabulary:

Corta un cartón de huevos en filas	Cut apart an egg carton into rows
Primero corta la tapa y las aletas del cartón de huevos	Cut the lid and flaps off of an egg carton first.
Pinta el exterior de la tira del cartón	Paint the outside of the egg cup strip
Voltea la tira para que pueda ver el exterior de las copas	Flip the strip over so that you can see the outside of the cups
Puedes pintar un extremo en rojo y el resto en verde para convertirlo en una oruga "muy hambrienta	You can paint one end red, and the rest of it green to make it a "very hungry" caterpillar.
Deja que la oruga se seque antes de continuar.	Let the caterpillar dry before moving on.
Haz dos agujeros en la primera copa.	Punch two holes in the first cup.
Elige un extremo para ser la cabeza, luego introduce dos agujeros en el medio para la antena.	Choose an end to be the head, then poke two holes in the middle for the antenna.
Corta un limpia pipas por la mitad, luego pásalo por los agujeros	Cut a pipe cleaner in half, then poke it through the holes
Gire el limpia pipas para hacer la antena	Twist the pipe cleaner to make the antenna
Dale a la oruga una cara	Design the caterpillar's face
Pegue dos ojos locos en la parte delantera, justo debajo de la antena.	Glue two googly eyes on the front end, just below the antenna.

SPANISH AT HOME · Erica Mirochnik · Minerva Ortega · Elizabeth García

LA RAYUELA

Learning objectives:

practice gross motor skills and numbers.

Instructions:

- Draw equal squares to be numbered. At the end a semi-circle that will be named "cielo".
- Stand in front of the first square and throw a small stone/bean inside it.
- Walk or jump each square in numerical order, with one foot, avoiding stepping on the square occupied by the stone.
- When you reach the 'cielo' you return in the same way but in order of descending numbers, to pick up the stone.

LOS DÍAS DE LA SEMANA

Learning objectives:

learn the days of the week in Spanish.

Materials needed:

- art supplies to build the train.

Instructions:

- cut out a train with seven wagons, one per day of the week
- Practice and learn the days of the week. Perform the game of exchanging the order of the days so that the children not only memorize visually but can recognize writing and sounds.

ADENTRO Y AFUERA

Learning objectives:

practice gross motor skills, vocabulary and spatial orientation.

Instructions:

- Mark a line or circle on the floor, either with a tape or small building blocks. On one side write the word "adentro" and on the other the word "afuera"

Vocabulary:

Say outloud: adentro, afuera, adentro, afuera... alternating languages so the child will jump to the indicated place.

TAPAS Y TAPITAS

Learning objectives:

practice fine motor skills, vocabulary.

Materials needed:

all kinds of plastics bottle caps, glue,

and canvases.

Instructions:

Give your child a drawing to be copied or ask him/her to draw and then fill it with the caps. You may want to do your own art project and work at the same time naming colors, shapes and other fun situations, in Spanish

GAMES 4 TO 6 YEARS OLD

Escondite

This is the popular Spanish version of "Hide and Seek". At the end of the count, the player says: "Escondidos o no, allá voy" and starts looking for the other players saying "te vi" when she/he finds them.

Vocabulario/Vocabulary: Escondidos o no, allá voy/ Hidden or not I'll go! Te vi/I saw you.

Bingo

You can create your own Bingo in Spanish with the theme of your choice or buy a game that includes the cards in Spanish. This is always a very fun and interesting game, kids love it!

Vocabulario/Vocabulary: Bingo/Bingo; Cartas/Cards; Ficha/Token.

¿Quién es quién?

Board games are especially welcomed in winter afternoons and holidays. The classic *Who is who?*, *Ladders game board* or *Connect four* are some of the many game options available in Spanish for this age.

Vocabulario/Vocabulary: ¿Quién es quién?/Who is who?, Connect Four/Cuatro en fila

El Juego de la Oca

This is a very popular board game in Spain. Two or more players move pieces around a track by rolling a die. The aim of the game is to be the first one reaching square number sixty-three.

Vocabulario/Vocabulary: Juego de la Oca/ Game of the Goose; Board Game/Juego de Mesa.

Carrera de obstáculos

Great outdoors game to exercise, run, jump and overcome the obstacles that we have included in the circuit. We take this opportunity to learn verbs in Spanish.

Vocabulario/Vocabulary: Carrera de obstáculos/ Obstacle course; Correr/To run; Saltar o Brincar/To jump or to Hop;

Juegos de memoria

A cards game that we can make ourselves and be ready to sit down in any corner of the house to train our memory while having fun.

Vocabulario/Vocabulary: Juego de memoria/ Memory game; Cartas/Cards.

Pilla-Pilla o Juego de perseguir (three or more players)

This is the classic "tag" game to play outside and it involves at least three or more players chasing other players in an attempt to "tag" or touch them. Before chasing each other they can start counting in Spanish.

Vocabulario/Vocabulary: Pillar/to tag; Jugador/Player; Normas/Rules; Tocar/To touch.

Pato, Pato, Ganso. (Three or more players)

Sitting in a circle one of the children (or an adult) sings and walks around the circle. While walking, he/she, is touching other people's head saying "Pato" "Pato" (the person can say several times"Pato") and suddenly says "Ganso" The child who has been touched in the head with the word "Ganso" tries to catch the one who has touched his head, both running around the circle, until the first kid sits in the empty space left by the one who chases him.

Vocabulario/Vocabulary: Pato, pato, ganso/ Duck, Duck, Goose.

 VOCABULARY

VOCABULARY

Números | Numbers:

Uno | One

Dos | Two

Tres | Three

Cuatro | Four

Cinco | Five

Seis | Six

Siete | Seven

Ocho | Eight

Nueve | Nine

Diez | Ten.

Colores | Colors:

Rojo | Red

Verde | Green

Azul | Blue

Amarillo | Yellow

Rosa o Rosado | Pink

Naranja o Anaranjado | Orange

Negro | Black

Blanco | White

Morado o Violeta | Purple

Gris | Grey

Café o Marrón | Brown.

Formas | Shapes:

Círculo | Circle

Cuadrado | Square

Triángulo | Triangle

Corazón | Heart

Estrella | Star

Cubo | Cube

Sentimientos | Feelings

Feliz | Happy

Triste | Sad

Enojado (boy) - Enojada (girl) | Mad

Asustado (boy) - Asustada (girl) | Scared

Frustrado (boy) - Frustrada (girl) | Frustrated

Tengo hambre | I'm hungry

Tengo sed | I'm thirsty

Estoy Cansado | I'm tired

Estoy enfermo | I'm sick

Estoy sorprendido (boy) - sorprendida (girl) | Excited.

SPANISH AT HOME · Erica Mirochnik · Minerva Ortega · Elizabeth García

VOCABULARY

Mi cuerpo | My body

Cara | Face

Ojos | Eyes

Boca | Mouth

Orejas | Ears

Nariz | Nose

Pelo | Hair

Dientes | Teeth

Manos | Hands

Pies | Feet

Brazos | Arms

Piernas | Legs.

Mi familia | My family

Mamá | Mom

Papá | Dad

Hermano | Brother

Hermana | Sister

Bebé | Baby

Abuelo | Grandfather

Abuela | Grandmother

Uncle | Tío

Aunt | Tía

Mascota | Pet

Perro | Dog

Gato | Cat

Pez | Fish.

Verbos | Verbs

Cantar | To sing

Hablar | To talk

Llorar | To cry

Besar | To kiss

Abrazar | To hug or to cuddle

Bailar | To dance

Dormir | To sleep

Gatear | To crawl

Comer | To eat

Beber | To drink

Descansar | To rest

Acunar | To cuddle

Comida | food

Leche | Milk

Agua | Water

Huevo | Egg

Puré | Puree

Sopa | Soup

Verdura o Vegetales | Vegetables

Carne | Meat

Pescado | Fish

Jugo - Zumo | Juice

SPANISH AT HOME · Erica Mirochnik · Minerva Ortega · Elizabeth García

RECIPES

RECIPES FROM SPAIN

TORTILLA DE PATATAS

Ingredientes:

- 2 patatas medianas
- 6 huevos
- Medía cebolla pequeña (opcional)
- 2 vasos de aceite de oliva
- Sal

Preparación:

1. Empieza pelando y lavando las dos patatas.
2. Corta las patatas en láminas finas.
3. Pica la cebolla en trocitos pequeños.
4. Pon el aceite a calentar en una sartén.
5. Añade las patatas y la cebolla (opcional) cuando el aceite esté muy caliente. Una vez fritas, sácala las patatas y la cebolla de la sartén y escúrrelas bien en un plato con un papel de cocina para que absorba el aceite.
6. Mezclar en un recipiente los huevos con las patatas y la cebolla ya frita y un poco de sal.
7. Con el aceite bien caliente, echa la mezcla de huevos-patatas en la sartén.
8. Cuando empiece a cuajar, después de unos 10 minutos, cubre la sartén con un plato y dale la vuelta. Realizamos el mismo proceso con el otro lado de la tortilla. Cuando esté dorada significa que está ¡lista para comer!

Recomendación:

En España la tortilla se suele comer acompañada en verano de un vaso de gazpacho o salmorejo y en invierno de una ensalada de tomates de la huerta picados o de unos pimientos verdes.

Vocabulario:

Tortilla de Patata/ Spanish Omelette; Patatas o papas/Potatoes; Huevos/Eggs; Cebolla/ Onion; Aceite de oliva /Olive Oil; Sal/Salt.

CROQUETAS DE POLLO

Ingredientes:

- 0,55 lb de pollo cocido o asado
- 0,33 lb de harina
- 33 oz de leche
- 2 huevos

- Mantequilla
- Una cebolla
- Aceite de oliva
- Sal

Preparación:

1. Trocea el pollo en trocitos muy pequeños y asegúrate que no queda ningún huesecito.

2. Por a calentar una sartén con una cucharada de mantequilla y cuando esté dorada añade la cebolla picada.

3. Una vez frita la cebolla a fuego lento, añade la harina y dale vueltas despacio con una cuchara de madera.

4. Añade el pollo y un poquito de sal a la mezcla.

5. Una vez dorada, saca la masa y ponla a reposar en una fuente durante 24 horas (puedes cubrirla con papel de aluminio para que no se reseque) y guárdala en la nevera/refrigerador.

6. Al día siguiente saca la bandeja de la nevera; bate en un recipiente un huevo y en otro plato pon el pan rallado.

7. Con ayuda de una cuchara coger porciones de la masa y con las manos dar forma ovalada. Una vez con la forma hecha, se pasa por el plato con el huevo y después por el plato con el pan rallado.

8. Una vez listas, pon aceite en la sartén y cuando esté muy caliente vas echando las croquetas. Fríelas a fuego medio hasta que estén doradas.

9. Sácalas del aceite, escúrrelas con un papel de cocina y ¡a disfrutar!

Vocabulario:

Pollo/Chicken; Harina/Flour; Leche/Milk; Huevos/Eggs; Mantequilla/Butter; Onio/Cebolla; Aceite de oliva/Olive oil; Sal/Salt.

GAZPACHO

Gazpacho may be one of the best known Spanish dishes. It originates from the South of Spain, particularly the region of Andalusia. It is a cold soup that is usually made from chopped raw vegetables (such as tomato, pepper, and cucumber) and that is served cold.

Ingredientes:

- 2 kilos de tomates maduros
- 1 pimiento rojo
- 1 pimiento verde
- Medio pepino
- Un trocito de pan
- Medio ajo
- Vinagre de vino blanco
- Aceite
- Sal
- Cominos

Preparación:

1. Lavar bien los tomates, el pepino y el pimiento y dejar escurrir.
2. Bate en un recipiente el pan con el resto de vegetales: tomates, pepino, pimiento y ajo (quítale el corazón para que no repita)
3. Una vez batido añade la sal, el aceite, el vinagre y una pizca de cominos (si van a tomar los niños puedes hacer una versión de gazpacho más suave sin ajo ni cominos).
4. Por último añade "toppins": trocitos de jamón serrano y huevo duro.
5. Sírvelo muy frío.

Vocabulario:

tomates/tomatos; pimientos/peppers; pepino/cucumber; vinage/vinager; cominos/cumin; huevo duro o huevo cocido/ boiled egg.

CHURROS

Ingredientes:

- 250 ml. de harina
- 250 ml. de agua
- 1 cuchara pequeña de sal
- Azúcar
- Manga pastelera

Preparación:

1. Calentar el agua en un cazo hasta que hierva.

2. Mezclar en un bol la harina y la sal. Cuando el agua empiece a hervir, añadir esta mezcla y retirar del fuego, mezclado bien para formar la masas.

3. Calentar abundante aceite en una sartén grande. Colocar la masa en una manga pastelera con boquilla ancha y echarla en la sartén dándole forma al churro.

4. Freír el churro hasta que esté dorado, sacarlo y dejar que escurra sobre papel de cocina. Para decorar espolvorear con azúcar.

5. Completa el desayuno o la merienda con una taza de chocolate caliente.

Vocabulario:

churros/churros; harina/flour; azúcar/sugar; cazo o cazuela/ pot; masa/dough; aceite/oil; chocolate caliente/hot cocoa.

RECIPES FROM ARGENTINA

BOMBONES DE CHOCOLATE

Ingredientes:

- 4 paquetes de galletas tipo "Maria" (tea biscuits)
- 1 taza de leche condensada
- Nesquick o chispas chocolate

Preparación:

1. Agregar la leche condensada y unificar hasta obtener una mezcla compacta. Poner esta mezcla en un molde y llevarla a la nevera unos 30 minutos.

2. Pasada esa medía hora, sacar la mezcla y comenzar a hacer las bolitas para luego rebozarlas con el cacao o chocolate.

Vocabulario:

bombones/truffles, taza/cup, agregar/to add, galletas/cookies, nevera/fridge, mezcla/to mix

ARROZ CON LECHE

Ingredientes:

- 1 litro de leche
- 250 g de arroz
- 100 g de azúcar
- 1 limón
- 1 canela en rama
- 2 cucharadas de canela en polvo

Preparación:

1. Hervir el arroz y dejarlo enfriar durante 10 minutos.

2. Calentar por separado la leche y el azúcar, revolviendo para que se disuelva.

3. Cuando la leche comience a hervir, agregar el arroz escurrido, la canela en rama y la piel de limón.

4. Dejar hervir a fuego bajo durante 15 minutos.

5. Ponerlo en una fuente o plato hondo y servir frío con canela en polvo.

Vocabulario:

arroz/rice; azucar/sugar; limón/lemon; canela en rama/cinnamon stick; polvo/powder; leche/milk; hervir/boil; enfriar/cool; calentar/heat; escurrir/drain; piel de limón/peel of a lemon.

MINI PIZZAS OR PIZZETAS

Ingredientes (6 unidades):

Dough:

- 25g levadura fresca
- 300 cc agua tibia
- 2 cuchara aceite de oliva
- 500g harina 0000 (harina de trigo)
- 1 cucharadita sal

Salsa:

- 1 taza puré de tomate
- 2 cuchara aceite de oliva
- sal y pimienta
- albahaca

Preparación:

1. Comience disolviendo la levadura en el agua tibia.
2. Agregar el aceite y mezclar.
3. Poner la harina y la sal en otro recipiente. Agregar la levadura y mezclar hasta formar una masa blanda. Cubrir con un film y dejar leudar.
4. Amasar la masa, dividirla en seis bollos y estirarlos en forma ovalada. Ponerlos en una fuente previamente aceitada y dejar que leuden unos 5-10 minutos.
5. Agregue la salsa con un pincel de cocina y ponga en el horno a 200C/395F durante 15 minutos.
6. Una vez que las pizzetas están cocidas agregue trozos de mozzarella y demás ingredientes a gusto (aceitunas, cebollas, tomates frescos, etc.) Llevar al horno durante unos 10 minutos.

Vocabulario:

masa/dough, harina/all-purpose flour; mezclar/to mix, leudar/to rise the dough, aceite/oil, amasar/knead, recipiente/container

RECIPES

EMPANADAS DE JAMÓN Y QUESO

Ingredientes:

- 220cc de agua
- 350gr de harina
- 80cl de aceite de oliva
- Sal

- 6 Lonjas jamón cocido
- Queso mozzarella
- 1 Huevo

Preparación:

1. Hervir el agua con la sal. Retiramos del fuego y agregar el aceite de oliva y la harina. Mezclar con una cuchara de madera hasta que no podamos seguir dando vueltas. Retiramos la masa de la olla y disponerla sobre un plato y dejar enfriar unos minutos.

2. Cubrir la mesada de la cocina con harina y poner la masa sobre la harina, amasar un poco la masa y separarla en 6 porciones iguales. Estiramos cada porción y la cortamos en forma de círculos de unos 16cm.

3. En cada disco de masa ponemos una lonja de jamón cocido troceado y el queso mozzarella.

4. Doblar el disco de masa sobre sí misma y con los dedos presionamos los laterales. Se puede hacer con un tenedor para que quede bien cerrada. Pintar con huevo cada empanada antes de cocinar.

5. Con el horno a 200°C calor hornear durante 35 minutos. Transcurrido el tiempo retiramos del horno y dejamos enfriar.

6. Estas empanadas pueden también freirse. El relleno puede variarse por carne, pollo, atún, espinacas, etc.

Vocabulario:

harina/all purpose flour; hervir/to boil; agua/water; masa/dough; mesada/counter; doblar/fold; jamón cocido/ham; huevo/egg; relleno/filling; hornear/to bake; freir/ to fry

🍴 RECIPES

 RECIPES FROM MEXICO

GUACAMOLE PARA TACOS

Ingredientes:

- 3 aguacates maduros medianos.
- 1 cebolla mediana (si puede ser, dulce)
- 1 un limón recién exprimido.

- Un chile serrano al gusto
- Cilantro fresco recién picado.
- Un poco de sal

Preparación:

1. El primer paso es agarrar los aguacates, hacerles un corte profundo por todo su perímetro y poder separar sus dos mitades sin ningún problema. Quitaremos el hueso y le sacaremos la pulpa con una cuchara, la cual iremos depositando en un plato hondo.

2. Cuando hayamos sacado toda la pulpa podremos machacarla toda con un tenedor hasta dejarlo con una masa cremosa, pero con cierta consistencia, como si se tratase de un puré.

3. Una vez machacado agregaremos el jugo de un limón recién exprimido para evitar que el aguacate se oxide y adquiera un color oscuro.

4. Por otro lado pelaremos la cebolla y picaremos la mitad en trozos muy finos, algo que podemos hacer o con un cuchillo muy afilado. La cebolla que hemos picado la incorporaremos al aguacate que tenemos en el plato ya triturado.

5. Picaremos el chile jalapeño o el chile serrano muy fino, procurando quitarle las semillas si no queremos que pique demasiado, lo incorporaremos al resto de ingredientes junto a un pizca de sal y a unas hojas de cilantro fresco recién picado.

Vocabulario:

Quitar/take out, pelar/ to peel, picar/to chop, triturar/to crush, picante/spicy, pizca/pinch, perimetro/perimeter

46

SPANISH AT HOME · Erica Mirochnik · Minerva Ortega · Elizabeth García

QUESADILLAS

Ingredientes:

- 150 gr de Queso que derrita
- 6 Tortillas de Maíz (120 gr)

Preparación:

1. Corte en tiras 150 gr de queso para fundir o derretir, después reserve.

2. Caliente en un comal a fuego medio 6 tortillas de maíz por unos 20 segundos por cada lado, hasta que estén suaves.

3. Ponga en cada tortilla unas tiras del queso que cortó.

4. Doble a la mitad todas las tortillas que puso en el comal.

5. Caliente las quesadillas por 1½ minutos aproximadamente por cada lado, hasta que el queso se haya derretido, mientras las quesadillas se calientan las puede aplastar ligeramente para que se derrita mejor el queso.

Vocabulario:

Queso/ cheese, fundir o derretir/to melt, comal/flat pan, tortilla/ unleavened corn flatbread, aplastar/to squash

SÁNDWICH DE ATÚN CON CHICHAROS

Ingredientes:

- 250 gramos de Chícharos (guisantes) cocidos
- 2 latas de atún en agua
- 1/4 de pieza de lechuga romana picada
- 1 pieza de pepino picado
- 2 cucharadas de mayonesa
- 1 pieza de limón (jugo)
- sal al gusto
- pimientas al gusto
- 8 rebanadas de pan integral

Preparación:

1. Prepare 250 gr de chícharos (guisantes) cocidos.

2. Drene el líquido de las latas de atún.

3. Mezcle todos los ingredientes, excluyendo el pan, y sazone con sal y pimienta.

4. Esparza ¼ de la ensalada de atún sobre una rebanada de pan, fresco o tostado, cubra con otra rebanada y corte diagonalmente por la mitad.

Vocabulario:

Mezclar/ To mix, Drenar/to drain, Excluir/ to exclude, chícharos/peas, esparcir/to spread, rebanada/slice, cucharadas/spoonful, latas/cans, lechuga/lettuce.

BIÓNICOS DE FRUTAS

Ingredientes (4 porciones):

- 1 taza de fresas, cortadas en cubitos
- 1 taza de melón, cortada en cubitos
- 1/4 taza de nueces pecanas picadas
- 1 taza de papaya, cortada en cubitos
- 1 Taza de piña, cortada en cubitos
- 1/3 taza de crema mexicana o crema agria
- 1/3 taza de yogur natural
- 1 cucharadita de vainilla
- 1/3 taza de leche condensada
- 1/4 taza de pasas
- 1/4 taza de coco rallado endulzado
- Miel (Opcional)
- 1/4 taza de granola natural

Preparación:

1. Mezcla suavemente la fruta cortada en un tazón mediano y póngala a un lado o colócala en el refrigerador para mantenerla fresca.
2. En un tazón pequeño, mezcla la crema, el yogur y la leche condensada.
3. Agrega la cucharadita de vainilla y mezcla bien.
4. Agrega 2 cucharadas de la mezcla cremosa en el fondo de 4 tazas o cuencos de postre. Divida la fruta en las tazas, justo antes de servir, vierta 2 cucharadas de la mezcla de crema sobre cada taza de fruta y decora con las nueces picadas, granola, pasas y coco rallado. Si lo prefieres, puedes dejar que todos adornen su taza de fruta a su gusto.
5. Agrega un poco de miel en la parte superior.

Vocabulario:

Taza/cup, tazón/bowl, miel/honey; vainilla/vanilla, mezclar/to mix, decorar/to decorate, dividir/to divide

BOOKS

BOOKS

SPANISH BOOKS FOR CHILDREN 0 TO 3 YEARS OLD

- **Siempre te querré** *by Robert Munsch.*
- **Mauro necesita un abrazo** *by David Melling.*
- **Nariz, naricita** *by Mar Benegas.*
- **Diez deditos de las manos y Diez deditos de los pies / Ten Little Fingers and Ten Little Toes bilingual board book** *by Mem Fox and Helen Oxenbury.*
- **El Pollo Pepe** *by Nick Denchfield.*
- **La oruga muy hambrienta** *by Eric Carle.*
- **El monstruo de colores** *by Anna Llenas.*
- **Colección Mi primer libro de... (formas, números, palabras...)** *by Eric Carle.*
- **Las manos de papá** *by Emile Jadoul.*
- **Las Diez Gallinas** *by Sylvia Dupuis.*
- **Cucú tras de mascotas** *by Francesca Ferri.*
- **Vamos a cazar un oso** *by Michael Rosen.*
- **Nacho ya usa el orinal/ Nacho Now Uses the Toilet** *by Liesbet Slegers.*
- **Donde esta el trapito de Iyoke?** *by Nathalie Dieterle.*
- **El Pequeño Hoo va a la Playa/ Little Hoo goes to the Beach (Bilingual Spanish English Edition)** *by Brenda Ponnay.*
- **Colección Pequeña Marina (La pequeña Marina dice ¡No! O La pequeña Marina va al parque)** *by Linne Bie.*
- **Colección Pequeño Edu (El pequeño Edu va al pedíatra / Little Edu Goes to the Pedíatrician)** *by Linne Bie.*
- **Vamos a la fiesta / Let's Have a Party** *by Guido Van Genechten.*
- **Paco y la orquesta** *by Magali Le Huche.*
- **El monstruo de colores** *by Anna Llenas.*
- **El Pez Arco Iris** *by Marcus Pfister.*
- **Zoológico Bilingüe /Bilingual Zoo** *By Erica Deery.*

 **BOOKS**

SPANISH BOOKS FOR CHILDREN 4 TO 6 YEARS OLD

- **Healthy Foods from A to Z/Comida Sana de La a A La Z** *by Stephanie Maze.*
- **Diez Deditos and Other Play Rhymes and Action Songs from Latin America** *by Jose-Luis Orozco and Elisa Kleven.*
- **El Grufalo** *by Julia Donaldson.*
- **El Día Que Los Crayones Renunciaron** *by Oliver Jeffers Drew Daywalt.*
- **La idea más maravillosa** *by Ashley Spires.*
- **Caperucita Roja** *by Brothers Grimm.*
- **Mi dragón y yo** *by David Biedrzycki.*
- **¿Cómo dicen te quiero los dinosaurios? o ¿Cómo dicen feliz cumpleaños los dinosaurios?** *by Jane Yolen.*
- **El autobús mágico en el cuerpo humano o El Autobús Mágico en El Sistema Solar** *by Joanna Cole and Bruce Degen.*
- **May I Please Have a Cookie? /¿Me puedes dar una galleta, por favor? (Bilingual Edition)** *by Jennifer E. Morris.*
- **Huevos verdes con jamón** *by Dr. Seuss.*
- **Un Pez, Dos Peces, Pez Rojo, Pez Azul (Spanish Edition),** *by Dr Seuss.*
- **¿Eres Mi Mama? (Spanish Edition),** *by Dr Seuss.*
- **Goodnight Moon / Buenas Noches, Luna (Spanish Edition),** *by Margaret Wise Brown.*
- **Perro grande... Perro pequeño / Big Dog... Little Dog (Spanish and English Edition),** *by P.D.Eastman.*
- **Opuestos (Opposites) (Spanish Edition),** *By Sandra Boynton.*
- **First 100 Words Bilingual (Spanish Edition) (Spanish)** *By Board book.*
- **My Big Book of Spanish Words Board book,** *by Rebecca Emberley.*
- **Animals: Animals (Bright Baby) (English and Spanish Edition),** *by Roger Priddy.*
- **Besos for Baby: A Little Book of Kisses,** *by Jen Arena.*
- **Head, Shoulders, Knees and Toes/Cabeza, Hombros, Piernas, Pies (Dual Language Baby Board Books- English/Spanish),** *by Annie Kubler.*
- **Cómo comer un arcoiris/How to eat a rainbow Bilingual version** *by Delia Berlín.*

APPS, BLOGS & WEBSITES

APPS, BLOGS & WEBSITES

APPS OR SOFTWARE

- **App spanish safari** www.learnsafari.com
- **App mundo lanugo** www.mundolanugo.com
- **App gus on the go** www.gusonthego.com
- **App juana la iguana** www.juanalaiguana.com
- **App fun spanish** www.studycat.net
- **DVD Brainy Baby Learn Spanish Language Classic Edition**
- **App mama lingua** www.mama-lingua.com
- **Como mola apps** https://www.comomola.rocks/#apps
- **CreAPPcuentos - Crea historias divertidas** http://www.creappcuentos.com/
- **Learn Spanish with Zoe** https://itunes.apple.com/es/app/learn-spanish-with-zoe
- **José Aprende** http://www.fundacionorange.es/aplicaciones/cuentos-visuales-jose-aprende
- **Termotic** http://tapp-mobile.com/es/termotic/

BLOGS & WEBSITES

- **Real Academia Española** http://www.rae.es/
- **Instituto Cervantes** http://www.cervantes.es/default.htm
- **Blog de Clara Pons Tierra en las manos** http://www.tierraenlasmanos.com/
- **Blog del enfermero de pediatría Armando Bastida** https://www.bebesymas.com/
- **Rejuega blog de Jessica Clemente** http://rejuega.com/
- **Think Bilingual Austin** http://austin.thinkbilingual.org/
- **Maritere Rodriguez Bellas** http://maritererodriguezbellas.com/
- **ELE para niños - Español Lengua Extranjera para Niños** http://www.eleparaninos.com/
- **Little Pim** https://www.littlepim.com/
- **Sésamo TV (Sesame Street in Spanish)** http://sesamo.com/
- **Dora la Exploradora (Dora the Explorer)** http://la.nickjr.tv/dora-la-exploradora
- **Aprendices Visuales** https://aprendicesvisuales.com/p/cuentos_aprendicesvisuales/
- **Reto Bilingüe** www.retobilingue.com
- **Infancia y Educación** www.infanciayeducacion.com
- **Mamás por el mundo** www.mamasporelmundo.com

HOLIDAYS AND CELEBRATIONS

HOLIDAYS AND CELEBRATIONS

 ## HOLIDAYS AND CELEBRATIONS IN ARGENTINA

- 1 de enero: **Año Nuevo**
- Fin de febrero: **Carnaval**
- 24 de marzo: **Día Nacional de la Memoria por la Verdad y la Justicia**
- 2 de abril: **Día del Veterano y de los Caídos en la Guerra de Malvinas (Falklands)**
- **Viernes Santo**
- 1 de mayo: **Día del Trabajador**
- 25 de mayo: **Día de la Revolución de Mayo**
- 3er domingo: **de junio Día del Padre**
- 20 de junio Día de la bandera: **Paso a la Inmortalidad del General Manuel Belgrano**
- 9 de julio: **Día de la Independencia**
- 20 de julio: **Día del Amigo**
- 3er domingo de agosto: **Día del Niño**
- 17 de agosto: **Paso a la Inmortalidad del General José de San Martín**
- 12 de octubre: **Día del Respeto a la Diversidad Cultural (originalmente llamado "Día de la Raza")**
- 3er domingo de octubre: **Día de la Madre**
- 20 de noviembre: **Día de la Soberanía Nacional**
- 8 de diciembre: **Día de la Inmaculada Concepción de María**
- 25 de diciembre: **Navidad**

Vocabulario/Vocabulary:

enero/January; febrero/February; marzo/March; abril/April; Mayo/May; junio/June; julio/July; agosto/August; septiembre/September; octubre/October; noviembre/November; diciembre/December; trabajador/worker; veterano/veteran; bandera/flag; Navidad/Christmas; año nuevo/New Year

HOLIDAYS AND CELEBRATIONS

HOLIDAYS AND CELEBRATIONS IN MEXICO

- 1 de Enero: **Año Nuevo**
- 6 de Enero: **Día de los Reyes Magos**
- 5 de Febrero: **Día de la Constitución Mexicana**
- 14 de Febrero: **Día de San Valentín**
- 24 de Febrero: **Día de la Bandera**
- 21 de Marzo: **Natalicio de Benito Juarez**
- **Semana Santa (**Jueves, Viernes Santos y Domingo de Resurrección**)**
- 30 de Abril: **Día del Niño**
- 1 de Mayo: **Día del trabajo**
- 5 de Mayo: **Batalla de Puebla**
- 10 de Mayo: **Día de la Madre**
- 3er domingo de junio: **Día del Padre**
- 16 de Septiembre: **Día de la independencia**
- 12 de Octubre: **Descubrimiento de América (Día de la Raza)**
- 2 de Noviembre: **Día de los muertos**
- 20 de Noviembre: **Revolución Mexicana**
- 12 de Diciembre: **Día de la virgen de Guadalupe**
- 24 de Diciembre: **Noche Buena**
- 25 de Diciembre: **Día de Navidad**

Vocabulario/Vocabulary:

Bandera/Flag, Natalicio/natal, Constitución/Constitution, Resurrección/Resurrection, independencia/Independence, Día de los muertos/Day of the Dead, Nochebuena/ Christmas Eve

SPANISH AT HOME · Erica Mirochnik · Minerva Ortega · Elizabeth García

HOLIDAYS AND CELEBRATIONS

 ## HOLIDAYS AND CELEBRATIONS IN SPAIN

- 1 de enero: **Año Nuevo**
- 6 de enero: **Cabalgata y noche de Los Reyes Magos**
- 14 de abril: **Viernes Santo**
- 1 de mayo: **Fiesta del Trabajo**
- 24 de junio: **San Juan**
- 15 de agosto: **Asunción de la Virgen**
- 12 de octubre: **Fiesta Nacional de España**
- 1 de noviembre: **Todos los Santos**
- 6 de diciembre: **Día de la Constitución**
- 8 de diciembre: **La Inmaculada**
- 25 de diciembre: **Navidad**

Otras celebraciones populares:

- **Las Fallas**, Valencia. Fiesta de la Hoguera de San Juan.
- **Semana Santa y La Feria de Abril**, Sevilla.
- **Día de Sant Jordi** en Barcelona celebrando su patrón y el Día Internacional del Libro, una jornada festiva llena de rosas, libros y actividades para toda la familia en las calles.
- **Fiesta de San Fermin**, Pamplona
- **El Camino de Santiago**. Peregrinación del Camino hasta la Catedral de Santiago que culmina como el 25 de julio con la celebración del Día del Apóstol Santiago y día grande de Galicia.

Vocabulario/Vocabulary:

Santo o Santa/ Saint, Cabalgata de Los Reyes Magos/Holy procession of the Three Kings/ Holidays/Días festivos, Celebrations/Celebraciones, Traditions/Tradiciones.

DID YOU KNOW...?

DID YOU KNOW...?

Although we share a common language, there are many variations to Spanish depending on the country.

Check these words:

Word in English	Spanish translation		
	México	Argentina	España
Boy and Girl	Niño y niño	Nene y Nena	Niño y niña
School	Escuela, colegio	Escuela, colegio	Escuela, Colegio
I love you	Te quiero	Te quiero	Te quiero
I miss you	Te extraño	Te extraño	Te echo de menos
I	Yo	Yo	Yo
You	Tú, usted (singular), ustedes (plural)	Vos, usted, ustedes (plural)	Tú (singular) vosotros (plural)
Pacifier or Binky	Chupón	Chupete	Chupete
Bib	Babero	Babero	Babero
Crib	Cuna	Cuna	Cuna
Baby's Bottle	Biberón, mamila	Mamadera	Biberón
Teacher	Maestro, profesor, miss	Maestro, profesor	Maestro, profesor
Red	Rojo	Rojo	Rojo
Brown	Café	Marrón	Marrón
Orange (color)	Anaranjado, naranja	Naranja	Naranja
Car	Carro, coche, auto.	Coche, auto	Coche
Embarrassment	Pena, vergüenza	Vergüenza	Vergüenza
Mad/Angry	Enojado	Enojado	Enfadado
To take/ To grab	Agarrar	Agarrar	Coger
Ball	Pelota, bola	Pelota	Pelota, balón
Bowling	Boliche	Bolos	Bolos
Stickers	Calcomanías	Calcomanías	Pegatinas
Babysitter	Niñera	Niñera	Canguro/Cuidadora/Niñera
Juice	Jugo	Jugo	Zumo

SPANISH AT HOME · Erica Mirochnik · Minerva Ortega · Elizabeth García

CONTACT

Erica Mirochnik

@mamasporelmundo
/Mamasporelmundo
/Mamasporelmundo
/Mamasporelmundo

Mamás por el Mundo
Consultoría para expatriadas

www.mamasporelmundo.com

Minerva Ortega

@retobilingue
/retobilingue
/retobilingue
/retobilingue

RETO BILINGÜE

www.retobilingue.com

Elizabeth García

@infanciayeducacion
/webdeinfanciayeducacion
/infanciayeducacion
/elizabethgarciacarro

Infancia Educación

www.infanciayeducacion.com